Major US Historical Wars

THE COLD WAR

John Ziff

Mason Crest
Philadelphia

Mason Crest
450 Parkway Drive, Suite D
Broomall, PA 19008
www.masoncrest.com

Printed and bound in the United States of America.
CPSIA Compliance Information: Batch #MUW2015.
For further information, contact Mason Crest at 1-866-MCP-Book.

3 5 7 9 8 6 4 2
Library of Congress Cataloging-in-Publication Data

ISBN: 978-1-4222-3355-9 (hc)
ISBN: 978-1-4222-8595-4 (ebook)

Major US Historical Wars series ISBN: 978-1-4222-3352-8

Picture Credits: Library of Congress: 13, 15, 20, 31, 45; National Archives: 17, 27, 39; Ronald Reagan Presidential Library : 51; used under license from Shutterstock, Inc.: 7, 10; 360b / Shutterstock.com: 1; United Nations photo: 34; U.S. Air Force photo: 22; U.S. Army Center of Military History: 43; U.S. Department of Defense: 36, 54; U.S. Department of Energy: 25; Wikimedia Commons: 48.

About the Author: John Ziff is a writer and editor who lives near Philadelphia.

TABLE OF CONTENTS

KEY ICONS TO LOOK FOR:

Text-dependent questions: These questions send the reader back to the text for more careful attention to the evidence presented there.

Words to understand: These words with their easy-to-understand definitions will increase the reader's understanding of the text, while building vocabulary skills.

Series glossary of key terms: This back-of-the book glossary contains terminology used throughout this series. Words found here increase the reader's ability to read and comprehend higher-level books and articles in this field.

Research projects: Readers are pointed toward areas of further inquiry connected to each chapter. Suggestions are provided for projects that encourage deeper research and analysis.

Sidebars: This boxed material within the main text allows readers to build knowledge, gain insights, explore possibilities, and broaden their perspectives by weaving together additional information to provide realistic and holistic perspectives.

Other Titles in This Series

Introduction

by Series Consultant
Jason Musteen

Why should middle and high school students read about and study American wars? Does doing so promote militarism or instill misguided patriotism? The United States of America was born at war, and the nation has spent the majority of its existence at war. Our wars have demonstrated both the best and worst of who we are. They have freed millions from oppression and slavery, but they have also been a vehicle for fear, racism, and imperialism. Warfare has shaped the geography of our nation, informed our laws, and it even inspired our national anthem. It has united us and it has divided us.

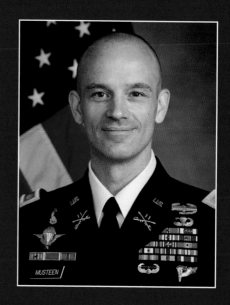

Lt. Col. Jason R. Musteen is a U.S. Army Cavalry officer and combat veteran who has held various command and staff jobs in Infantry and Cavalry units. He holds a PhD in Napoleonic History from Florida State University and currently serves as Chief of the Division of Military History at the U.S. Military Academy at West Point. He has appeared frequently on the History Channel.

Valley Forge, the *USS Constitution*, Gettysburg, Wounded Knee, Belleau Wood, Normandy, Midway, Inchon, the A Shau Valley, and Fallujah are all a part of who we are as a nation. Therefore, the study of America at war does not necessarily make students or educators militaristic; rather, it makes them thorough and responsible. To ignore warfare, which has been such a significant part of our history, would not only leave our education incomplete, it would also be negligent.

For those who wish to avoid warfare, or to at least limit its horrors, understanding conflict is a worthwhile, and even necessary, pursuit. The American author John Steinbeck once said, "all war is a symptom of man's failure as a thinking animal." If Steinbeck is right, then we must think.

And we must think about war. We must study war with all its attendant horrors and miseries. We must study the heroes and the villains. We must study the root causes of our wars, how we chose to fight them, and what has been achieved or lost through them. The study of America at war is an essential component of being an educated American.

Still, there is something compelling in our military history that makes the study not only necessary, but enjoyable, as well. The desperation that drove Washington's soldiers across the Delaware River at the end of 1776 intensifies an exciting story of American success against all odds. The sailors and Marines who planted the American flag on the rocky peak of Mount Suribachi on Iwo Jima still speak to us of courage and sacrifice. The commitment that led American airmen to the relief of West Berlin in the Cold War inspires us to the service of others. The stories of these men and women are exciting, and they matter. We should study them. Moreover, for all the suffering it brings, war has at times served noble purposes for the United States. Americans can find common pride in the chronicle of the Continental Army's few victories and many defeats in the struggle for independence. We can accept that despite inflicting deep national wounds and lingering division, our Civil War yielded admirable results in the abolition of slavery and eventual national unity. We can celebrate American resolve and character as the nation rallied behind a common cause to free the world from tyranny in World War II. We can do all that without necessarily promoting war.

In this series of books, Mason Crest Publishers offers students a foundation for the study of American wars. Building on the expertise of a team of accomplished authors, the series explores the causes, conduct, and consequences of America's wars. It also presents educators with the means to take their students to a deeper understanding of the material through additional research and project ideas. I commend it to all students and to those who educate them to become responsible, informed Americans.

Chapter 1:

ORIGINS OF THE COLD WAR

If you were a student during the 1950s, your school might have shown you a short film featuring Bert the Turtle. In the opening sequence, the cartoon character—walking upright and wearing a bowtie and round hat—strolls down a tree-lined lane. A monkey in a tree soon dangles a lit stick of dynamite above Bert. An explosion occurs. But Bert emerges unhurt. That's because, as a catchy song explains:

When the Soviet Union developed atomic weapons, Americans worried about the possibility of nuclear war. In many communities, fallout shelters like the one pictured above were constructed in the basements of public buildings during the 1950s. These were places where people could go to protect themselves in case of a nuclear attack.

He did what we all must learn to do,
You and you and you and you:
Duck and cover.

Imagining the Unimaginable

The film *Duck and Cover* was supposed to reinforce safety drills that kids practiced in school. Obviously, no one was really worried about monkeys with explosives. The actual concern was an atomic bomb attack.

Such an attack might come without warning. The first sign would be an intense flash of light, brighter than the sun. If you saw that flash, you were taught to drop to the ground immediately. You were taught to cover your head with your hands and forearms. That might save you from being killed by flying debris. For the detonation of the bomb would produce a massive shock wave. Tornado-speed winds would follow. Whipped through the air by these forces, broken glass, rubble, and all kinds of everyday objects would become lethal projectiles.

Duck and Cover assured its viewers that if they stayed down until this danger had passed, they might live through an attack with atomic weapons.

 # WORDS TO UNDERSTAND IN THIS CHAPTER

capitalism—an economic system that permits the ownership of private property and allows individuals and companies to compete for their own economic gain.

communism—a political and economic system that champions the elimination of private property, promotes the common ownership of goods, and typically insists that the Communist Party has sole authority to govern.

Kremlin—the top leadership of the Soviet Union.

superpower—an extremely powerful state; one of a few states that dominate an era.

The film didn't delve into the nightmarish world that would await survivors, though. In a full-scale attack, many cities and towns would be leveled. Fires would burn out of control for days or weeks. Millions of people would have been killed instantly. Millions more would be mortally injured. Many people who at first appeared unhurt would have been exposed to dangerous levels of radiation. Their likely fate was a slow, painful death.

For a long time, it seemed entirely possible that this horrific scenario might happen. That's because the world's two most powerful countries, the United States and the Union of Soviet Socialist Republics (USSR), were locked in a tense, high-stakes conflict. It was known as the Cold War. Most historians say the Cold War lasted from 1947 until 1991.

A Different Kind of Struggle

The Cold War was different from other wars in the nation's history. In fact, it wasn't really a war in the way we typically use that term. The armed forces of the United States and the Soviet Union, as the USSR was also called, didn't fight each other directly.

The Cold War is best understood as a political struggle—albeit one that was extremely wide ranging. The United States and the Soviet Union, the world's two *superpowers*, vied for influence across the globe. They sought to enlist other countries as allies or, at the very least, to discourage other countries from siding with their adversary. The superpowers' confrontation played out in various arenas—military, economic, diplomatic, and even cultural.

The term *cold war*—as distinguished from a "hot war," in which there is actual fighting—was coined by the British writer George Orwell in 1945. Two years later, the American journalist Walter Lippmann popularized the term as a way of describing U.S.-Soviet relations.

Allies or Adversaries?

During World War II (1939–45), the United States and the Soviet Union had been allies in the fight against Nazi Germany. But cracks in the relationship appeared even before the war was over.

By February 1945, Germany's defeat was all but certain. The Soviet Red Army was pushing in on Germany from the east. American, British, and other Allied forces were closing in from the west.

Against this backdrop, the leaders of the three main Allied nations met at Yalta, a Soviet resort town by the Black Sea. The so-called Big Three—President Franklin D. Roosevelt of the United States; Winston Churchill, prime minister of the United Kingdom; and Joseph Stalin, premier of the Soviet Union—discussed a variety of issues at the Yalta Conference. Among the most important was the future of Europe.

The Big Three agreed to jointly oversee Germany after its surrender.

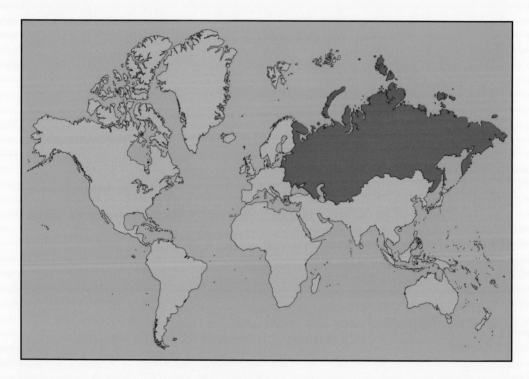

The Soviet Union, marked in red on this map, was the largest country, by area, in the world. As World War II ended, American leaders feared the Soviets would spread their Communist ideology throughout Europe and Asia.

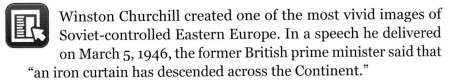

Winston Churchill created one of the most vivid images of Soviet-controlled Eastern Europe. In a speech he delivered on March 5, 1946, the former British prime minister said that "an iron curtain has descended across the Continent."

Germany would be divided into American, British, and Soviet zones of occupation. A French zone of occupation would later be carved out of the American and British zones. The Yalta Conference affirmed "the right of all people to choose the form of government under which they will live." In keeping with that principle, Stalin promised to allow free elections in countries the Red Army liberated from the Nazis.

But Stalin soon made it clear that he had no intention of living up to his promises, at least not in Poland. He insisted on having a "friendly" government there. This, he said, was necessary to help protect the USSR against invasion from the west. Germany had launched such an invasion, largely through Poland, in 1941.

Was Stalin's position on Poland reasonable? Or was it a sign he couldn't be trusted? American officials were divided on that question.

Some friction between the United States and the Soviet Union seemed unavoidable, though. The guiding principles of the two countries were completely at odds.

Two Systems

The American system of liberal democracy emphasized individual rights and freedoms. These included political rights (such as the right to vote and the right to run for public office) and civil rights (such as freedom of speech, the right to assemble peaceably, and freedom of the press).

Capitalism, the basis of the U.S. economy, also rested on individual freedom. Under capitalism, people are free to own or invest in a business. Business owners are free (within certain limits) to run their enterprises as they see fit. Individuals may accumulate as much property and wealth as they are able.

The Soviet system was underpinned by a theory called **communism**. It held that capitalism inevitably led to the exploitation of workers. It also held that capitalism was doomed, because workers would eventually revolt. Communism envisioned a future world in which there was full economic equality. There would be no rich and no poor. Each person would receive what he or she needed.

But communism couldn't come immediately after the workers' revolution in a particular country. First there needed to be a period of transition. During this period, the society would be organized under a type of socialism. The state would own factories and other places of work. It would run the economy not for the profit of individuals but for the benefit of all society, though some inequality would continue to exist.

Under the Soviet form of socialism, economic decision making was highly centralized. A committee of top officials at the **Kremlin**—the government complex in the capital city of Moscow—decided which goods the Soviet economy would produce, and in what quantities. State-owned factories were then charged with producing those goods.

In the USSR, the Communist Party claimed sole and absolute authority to govern. Opposing political parties weren't allowed. Nor was criticism of the government tolerated. Citizens who questioned Soviet policies were subject to harsh punishment. Communists claimed to be advancing economic justice. And that, they argued, was the most important goal. It trumped the political and civil rights emphasized by the United States and other Western nations.

A Meeting at Potsdam

At the most basic level, the U.S. and Soviet systems were in tension. But did that mean the two countries couldn't find ways to minimize conflict between them? They had, after all, put aside their differences to fight a

Clement Atlee of Great Britain, Harry Truman of the United States, and Joseph Stalin of the Soviet Union meet at Potsdam, Germany, in July 1945. During the Potsdam Conference, Truman told Stalin that the United States had developed a "powerful new weapon"—atomic bombs, which would soon be dropped on Japan.

common enemy during World War II. Might practical considerations also lead them to seek some accommodation in the postwar period?

On July 17, 1945, the Potsdam Conference opened. It brought together, once again, the leaders of the Allied nations. Harry S. Truman now represented the United States, having become president upon Roosevelt's death on April 12. The agenda at Potsdam focused largely on what to do with defeated Germany.

The Germans had surrendered more than two months earlier. But World War II wasn't quite over, as the Allies hadn't yet obtained Japan's surrender.

At Potsdam, President Truman met Joseph Stalin. His impressions of the Soviet leader were positive. "He is straightforward," Truman wrote. "Knows what he wants and will compromise when he can't get it."

Truman understood that dealing with the Soviet Union wouldn't be easy. In the end, though, he believed the USSR would go along with American plans for postwar Europe. He thought Stalin would see that the Soviet Union had little to gain from a confrontation with the United States.

The president's optimism was bolstered by news he'd received on the eve of the Potsdam Conference. On July 16, scientists working on a top-secret program called the Manhattan Project successfully tested a new type of weapon. In a remote area of New Mexico, they detonated the world's first atomic bomb. The explosion was unlike anything seen before. It carried the force of about 21 kilotons (21,000 tons) of dynamite.

The Manhattan Project had overcome enormous scientific and engineering hurdles to create the atomic bomb. Scientists and engineers in the USSR would eventually figure out how to do so as well. But many American military experts believed that would take at least a decade. In the meantime, the United States would be the only country to possess the most destructive weapon ever created.

Soviet leaders would have to take into account the U.S. monopoly on atomic weapons. President Truman thought the Soviets would be a bit more cooperative as a result. Secretary of State James Byrnes had greater expectations. Byrnes believed that "in the last analysis, [the atomic bomb] would control" Soviet behavior.

In August 1945, the world witnessed the terrible power of the new weapon. The United States used two atomic bombs to destroy two Japanese cities, Hiroshima and Nagasaki. More than 100,000 people were killed immediately. Tens of thousands would die later from the effects of radiation. Japan announced its surrender five days after the Nagasaki bombing.

The atomic bomb used a process called nuclear fission. Fission is a chain reaction during which the nuclei (centers) of uranium or plutonium atoms are split apart. A tremendous amount of energy is released as a result.

Growing Concerns

The atomic bomb failed to affect Soviet decision making the way Byrnes, or even Truman, anticipated. The Soviet Union wasn't cowed. It showed little inclination to cooperate with the United States. It certainly wasn't about to let Washington dictate the terms of world affairs.

Soviet leaders seemed determined to install Communist governments not only in Poland, but also in Romania and Bulgaria. And the Kremlin's designs weren't limited to Eastern Europe. Soviet troops tried to set up a puppet government in northern Iran. The Soviet Union also made clear its intention to annex two provinces in Turkey. It demanded from Turkey special rights in the Turkish Straits, waters that connect the Black Sea and the Mediterranean Sea.

These developments alarmed members of the Truman administration. There was a growing sense that the Soviet Union couldn't be trusted. But what did the Kremlin ultimately want? And how should the United States deal with the USSR?

The Long Telegram

In early 1946, the U.S. State Department asked a diplomat named George Kennan to explain Soviet actions and intentions. Kennan, the head of the U.S. Embassy in Moscow, responded with a 17-page telegram. The document was dubbed the "Long Telegram." Its influence on American policy would be profound.

According to Kennan, Soviet leaders thought a clash for control of the world economy was coming. It would pit the "socialist center" (the USSR) against the "capitalist center" (mainly

George Kennan was an American diplomat who served as ambassador to the Soviet Union in the 1940s. He helped to develop the U.S. foreign policy approach known as "containment" during the early days of the Cold War.

the United States). Soviet leaders—and particularly Stalin—believed that peaceful coexistence between the two sides was impossible in the long term.

Thus, Kennan said, the USSR would do everything it could to weaken the United States. It would try to sow discord within American society. It would try to turn U.S. allies against one another. It would aid Communist groups and political parties in Western democratic nations. It would encourage and support violent revolutions in poor countries.

Kennan called the Soviet challenge "undoubtedly [the] greatest task our diplomacy has ever faced." But he believed the United States could meet that challenge without a war. The Kremlin, he noted, didn't take unnecessary risks. Soviet leaders were inclined to back down when faced with a strong foe that showed a willingness to use force. And, as Kennan would later point out, repeated frustrations should lead the USSR to moderate its behavior.

The Long Telegram helped clarify the Truman administration's thinking about the Soviet Union. The result was a policy called containment. Its goal was to prevent the spread of communism around the world.

The stage was now set for the Cold War.

 ## TEXT-DEPENDENT QUESTIONS

1. Who was the Soviet Union's leader during World War II?
2. What was the Manhattan Project?
3. What was the "Long Telegram"? What policy did it help give rise to?

 ## RESEARCH PROJECT

The USSR was founded in December 1922. Use a library or the Internet to research how this happened. Then do a timeline. Include important events from 1905 until the death of Vladimir Lenin in 1924.

Chapter 2:

OPENING MOVES

On March 12, 1947, President Truman spoke before a special joint session of Congress. Some historians point to the speech as the start of the Cold War.

Relations with the USSR had gotten steadily worse over the previous year. American officials were especially upset by the Soviet rejection of the Baruch Plan. The Baruch Plan was a proposal the United States put forward in the United Nations, an international organization formed in

President Harry S. Truman (left) discusses the U.S. plan to provide financial assistance to help European countries rebuild after World War II. The advisors pictured include George C. Marshall (second from left), whose name became synonymous with the plan; and Marshall Plan administrators Paul Hoffman and Averell Harriman.

WORDS TO UNDERSTAND IN THIS CHAPTER

coup—the overthrow of a government by a small group, usually through violence or the threat of violence.

doctrine—a statement of fundamental government policy, particularly with regard to foreign affairs.

1945. It called for the creation of an international agency to ensure the peaceful development of atomic energy. The United States pledged to get rid of its stockpile of atomic bombs after the agency was up and running. But the Soviet Union insisted that the United States give up its bombs first. Only then would the USSR consider the Baruch Plan.

For many American policy makers, this marked a turning point. It was naïve, they concluded, to hold out hope the Kremlin might play a constructive role in international affairs. That pessimism formed the backdrop to Truman's March 12 speech.

The Truman Doctrine

The president had a specific purpose in going before Congress. He wanted approval for $400 million in economic and military aid. The aid would go to two countries: Greece and Turkey.

In Greece, Communist-led rebels were fighting to overthrow the government. The Truman administration hoped U.S. aid would enable the Greek government to defeat the rebels. But the administration also feared that the unrest in Greece might spill over into neighboring Turkey. And Communist-inspired turmoil there could threaten the stability of the entire Middle East. Aid to Turkey would help ensure that didn't happen.

The president and his advisers believed the USSR was supporting the Greek Communist rebels. It wasn't. But that fact wouldn't have made any difference in the way Truman framed the Greek crisis.

In his speech, the president identified a threat to free nations from certain "aggressive movements." By this he meant Communist movements. He said these movements had as their goal the establishment of totalitarian regimes. A totalitarian regime is a government—like the Soviet government under Stalin—that seeks to control every aspect of its citizens' lives. The methods of such a regime, in Truman's words, include "terror and oppression, a controlled press and radio, fixed elections, and the suppression of personal freedoms."

A Communist dictatorship could be imposed on a free nation through foreign interference or coercion. That, Truman suggested, was what the Soviet Union had been doing in Eastern European countries. But a Communist dictatorship might also be imposed from *within* a country. Under the right circumstances, even a relatively small group of Communist rebels could overthrow a government. And once it held the reins of power, such a group might do away with democratic institutions.

In Truman's view, a Communist dictatorship that resulted from a home-grown revolution was just as unacceptable as a Communist dictatorship that came about through Soviet coercion. Both threatened world peace. Both undermined U.S. security.

In his speech before Congress, the president offered a prescription for dealing with the problem. "I believe that it must be the policy of the United States," he declared, "to support free peoples who are resisting attempted subjugation by armed minorities or by outside pressures." That sentence expressed what became known as the Truman *Doctrine*.

The Truman Doctrine represented a dramatic shift in U.S. foreign policy. Historically, the United States had not sought a leading role in world affairs. It mostly avoided getting involved in conflicts outside the Western Hemisphere. But the Truman Doctrine committed the United States to giving assistance to any free country under threat of a Communist take-over. And that threat could be internal or external. Such a commitment could easily draw the United States into conflicts all across the globe.

The Marshall Plan

By 1947, World War II had been over for two years. But much of Europe still lay in ruins. European economies were wrecked. Many countries faced the prospect of famine.

On June 5, 1947, George C. Marshall delivered a speech calling for U.S. aid to rebuild Europe. Marshall was the secretary of state. His proposal, which had been developed by State Department officials, was popularly known as the Marshall Plan. Officially called the European Recovery Program, it was passed by Congress and signed into law by President Truman in April 1948.

Over a four-year period, the Marshall Plan gave almost $13 billion in aid to countries in Western Europe. This aid included food, fuel, machinery, and technical assistance. The economies of Western Europe rebounded.

The Marshall Plan was a humanitarian program. It improved living conditions for millions of people. At the same time, though, the plan served the U.S. policy of containment. Officials in the Truman administration were convinced that communism held its greatest appeal where poverty and misery abounded. As George Kennan observed, "World communism is like [a] malignant parasite which feeds only on diseased tissue."

The Marshall Plan had been open to all European countries. But Stalin denounced the program. He said it was an American ploy to dominate Europe economically. The Soviet Union prevented the nations of Eastern Europe from participating in the Marshall Plan.

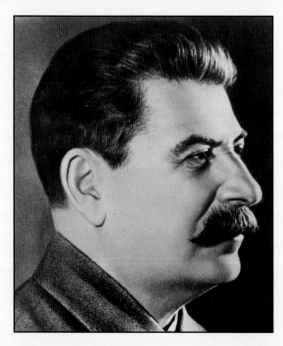

Joseph Stalin, leader of the Soviet Union from 1924 until his death in 1953, supported communist governments in Eastern European countries like Poland, Czechoslovakia, Hungary, Romania, Bulgaria, and East Germany.

The government of Czechoslovakia had signaled its openness to accept-
ing U.S. aid. But in early 1948, the Kremlin sponsored a *coup* that brought
a hard-line Communist regime to power in Czechoslovakia. That country—like Poland, Romania, Bulgaria, and Hungary—was now under the
control of the USSR.

The German Question

Another flashpoint in the budding Cold War soon emerged. At issue was
the future of Germany.

By 1947, the British occupation zone of Germany was experiencing
serious problems. With its own economy in bad shape, the UK didn't
have the funds to administer its zone effectively. So in September 1947,
the U.S. and British occupation zones were combined. A short time later,
France folded its sector into the combined occupation zone.

Still, the economic situation in Germany was dire. One factor ham-
pering a recovery was the lack of a common currency. Different money
was used in different places, which stifled commerce. In February 1948,
American and British officials proposed that a single currency be used
throughout Germany.

The Soviet Union promptly rejected the proposal. Many historians
believe the USSR wanted to keep the German people desperately poor.
That way, Germans would be more inclined to accept communism.

But the United States and its allies went ahead and created a common
currency for the Western occupation zone. It was introduced on June
18, 1948. About a week later, the USSR set up a blockade of West Berlin.

Berlin was the former capital of Germany. Like the rest of Germany,
the city had been divided after World War II. The Soviet sector covered
the eastern half of Berlin. The western half was made up of U.S., British,
and French sectors.

But Berlin lay deep within the Soviet occupation zone of Germany. That
enabled the USSR to cut off all rail, river, and highway routes into West

Residents of West Berlin watch as a U.S. cargo plane delivers desperately needed supplies during the Berlin Airlift. During the airlift, U.S. Air Force planes brought more than 2.3 million tons of cargo—mostly coal and food—into Berlin, which was blockaded by Soviet forces.

Berlin. The blockade, Soviet leaders believed, would leave the United States and its partners with only two options. Either they would agree to turn over their sectors in West Berlin to the USSR, or they would have to watch as residents of West Berlin starved.

But President Truman settled on a third option. Against the advice of many members of his administration—who thought it might provoke a war with the Soviet Union—Truman approved a massive airlift.

Every day for nearly 11 months, American and British cargo planes landed round the clock in West Berlin. They provided all the food, fuel, and other supplies 2 million people needed to survive. The Berlin airlift included some very tense moments. Soviet fighter jets harassed the supply flights, at times even firing close to cargo planes. But no planes were shot down. And on May 12, 1949, the USSR finally lifted the blockade of West Berlin.

The United States and its allies had concluded that the Soviet Union would never permit Germany to be reunified. So they decided to create an independent nation from the Western occupation zone. The Federal Republic of Germany, or West Germany, was founded on May 23, 1949.

The USSR responded by creating a new Communist country from its zone of occupation. The German Democratic Republic, or East Germany, was founded October 7, 1949.

Momentous Events

Earlier in the year, growing fears over possible Soviet aggression in Western Europe had led to the formation of a new military alliance. At its founding on April 4, 1949, the North Atlantic Treaty Organization (NATO) included 10 member countries from Western Europe. These were Belgium, Denmark, France, Iceland, Italy, Luxembourg, the Netherlands, Norway, Portugal, and the United Kingdom. They were joined by Canada and the United States.

NATO was based on the idea of collective security. An attack on any member would be treated as an attack on all members. For the United States, NATO marked a milestone. Never before had the country entered a military alliance outside the Western Hemisphere during peacetime.

The formation of NATO was rightly seen as a major victory in the U.S. effort to contain Soviet expansion. But it was offset by a pair of events that

Besides the United States and the USSR, six countries developed nuclear weapons during the Cold War: the United Kingdom (1952), France (1960), China (1964), India (1974), Israel (date unknown), and South Africa (possibly 1979). South Africa later gave up its nuclear weapons.

TEXT-DEPENDENT QUESTIONS

1. Who said, "I believe that it must be the policy of the United States to support free peoples who are resisting attempted subjugation by armed minorities or by outside pressures"?

2. Name the U.S. program to rebuild war-torn Europe.

3. What was NATO, and why was it formed?

RESEARCH PROJECT

The Soviet Union and the United States (as well as their respective allies) devoted significant resources to spying on the other side. Learn about a Cold War spy case or incident, then write a one- or two-page report. Make sure to describe who was involved, what was done, and why it was significant. Some possibilities: Julius and Ethel Rosenberg, the Cambridge Five, the Berlin Tunnel, Francis Gary Powers and the U-2 incident, Dmitri Polyakov, Aldrich Ames.

took place during the latter half of 1949. Those events stunned American policy makers and the general public alike.

On August 29, the USSR successfully tested an atomic bomb. The U.S. nuclear-weapons monopoly had come to an end after just four years. As American officials would discover, the Soviet atomic program had been greatly aided by spies inside the Manhattan Project.

Scarcely a month after the Soviet nuclear test, another country became Communist. And it wasn't just any country. It was China, the world's most populous nation. Chinese Communist forces had triumphed in a long civil war. Their leader, Mao Zedong, announced the founding of the People's Republic of China on October 1, 1949.

As the 1950s began, nearly one-third of the world's people lived under Communist rule. Communism appeared to be on the march.

Chapter 3:

HOT WAR, H-BOMBS, AND HYSTERIA ON THE HOME FRONT

By 1950, containment of the Soviet Union had become the primary goal of U.S. foreign policy. But what was the best way to achieve that end? As yet no clear agreement had emerged.

The first American test of a thermonuclear weapon—better known as a hydrogen bomb, or H-bomb, occurred in 1952. This type of weapon was hundreds of times more powerful and destructive than the atomic bombs dropped on Japan in 1945.

NSC-68

In January 1950, President Truman asked for a full review of American strategy. The task fell to a group within the State Department. In April, the group's findings were presented in a top-secret report. It's referred to as NSC-68.

NSC-68 painted a stark picture. The Kremlin, it said, was determined "to impose its absolute authority over the rest of the world" through military conquest. The report concluded that the only way to deter the USSR was for the United States to embark on a huge military buildup. That buildup, according to NSC-68, should include an increase in the size of the U.S. armed forces. It should include the development of new weapons systems. It should include an expansion of the American nuclear arsenal.

Not everyone in the Truman administration agreed with the conclusions of NSC-68. Truman himself was concerned about the cost of the proposed military buildup. But his reservations soon dissolved. U.S. military spending would nearly triple between 1950 and 1953, and the United States and the USSR slipped into a decades-long arms race. The turning point was a surprise invasion on the Korean Peninsula.

War in Korea

On June 25, 1950, more than 130,000 North Korean soldiers swept across the 38th parallel. That line of latitude formed the border between Communist North Korea and U.S.-allied South Korea. Kim Il-sung, the dictator

 WORDS TO UNDERSTAND IN THIS CHAPTER

>   *bloc*—a group of nations united by a common purpose, or formally allied by a treaty or agreement.
>
>   *Eastern bloc*—the Soviet-aligned Communist countries of Eastern Europe.

Two days after North Korean forces invaded South Korea in June 1950, President Harry S. Truman committed American troops to defend South Korea. Here, U.S. soldiers and a tank take a defensive position, 1950.

of North Korea, was determined to unify the Korean Peninsula under his rule. Kim had received the Kremlin's approval for an invasion of the South. He'd also gotten a green light from China.

The United Nations Security Council took up the matter of North Korea's invasion. A resolution was quickly approved. It called on UN member states to send troops to help South Korea. Sixteen countries responded. The UN forces would be under the overall command of the United States, which contributed nearly 85 percent of the personnel.

By early August 1950, North Korean forces controlled almost all of the Korean Peninsula. UN forces clung to a small defensive line around the port of Pusan. Then, in mid-September, UN troops landed behind enemy lines at Inchon. In danger of being cut off and surrounded, the North Koreans began a headlong retreat.

Within a couple months, UN forces seemed on the verge of total victory. They'd pushed well past the 38th parallel. And the UN commander, American general Douglas MacArthur, was determined take the entire peninsula. MacArthur planned to drive the North Koreans across the Yalu River into China.

In November, as UN forces approached the Yalu, about 300,000 Chinese soldiers entered the war on the side of North Korea. They drove UN forces back. UN forces eventually counterattacked. The fighting was brutal. But neither the Communists nor the UN forces could gain the upper hand.

Finally, in June 1953, an armistice was signed. It ended the fighting. The border between North and South Korea was nearly where it had been before the war started. But more than 2 million Koreans were dead. China had lost an estimated 600,000 soldiers. American dead totaled more than 36,000. The first "hot war" the United States fought to contain communism had proved costly indeed.

Hydrogen Bombs

On November 1, 1952, as the Korean War raged, the United States tested a new weapon. Code-named Ivy Mike, it vaporized a small island in the Pacific Ocean.

Like the atomic bomb, Mike was a nuclear device. But it harnessed another process: fusion. Using an atomic bomb as the trigger, Mike fused together nuclei of a form of hydrogen. Fusion is what powers the sun.

The amount of energy released by fusion is staggering. The Ivy Mike hydrogen-bomb test produced a blast equivalent to 10.4 megatons (10.4 million tons) of dynamite. It was nearly a thousand times more powerful than the atomic bomb that destroyed Hiroshima.

The U.S. hydrogen-bomb monopoly didn't last long. In August 1953, the USSR tested its own H-bomb.

The first hydrogen bombs (also called thermonuclear weapons) were too large to be deployed. There was no way to deliver them to a target. But by the end of 1955, both superpowers had designed H-bombs that were compact enough to be carried on planes.

The "New Look"

Throughout the 1950s, the United States held a large advantage over the Soviet Union in the number of nuclear weapons in its arsenal. The administration of President Dwight D. Eisenhower (1953–1961) placed great emphasis on maintaining that advantage. That was part of Eisenhower's "New Look" foreign policy.

The New Look was driven largely by economics. Defending all the nation's allies with conventional (non-nuclear) forces would have required the United States to maintain a large army. American troops might have to be deployed in many parts of the world. That would be very expensive. Eisenhower and his advisers wanted a cheaper alternative. So they threatened to respond to Communist aggression against the United States or any of its allies with "massive retaliation" using nuclear weapons.

Attempting to deter potential enemies in this manner was risky. It assumed no one would test U.S. willingness to follow through on the nuclear threat. "The ability to get to the verge without getting into the war is the necessary art," noted Secretary of State John Foster Dulles. "If you cannot master it, you inevitably get into war. If you try to run away from it, if you are scared to go to the brink, you are lost."

Witch-Hunt on the Home Front

As the Cold War unfolded, a climate of fear took hold in the United States. Many Americans believed that the struggle against world communism was being lost. It was clear, too, that some Americans wanted to help the Soviet Union. That was demonstrated most shockingly by the exposure of the spy ring that had passed atomic-bomb secrets to the USSR.

Did the Soviet Union have other agents inside the U.S. government? It was a reasonable question. But attempts to ferret out actual disloyalty turned into "witch-hunts." Thousands of Americans who had done nothing illegal were swept up in the anticommunist hysteria. An estimated 10,000 to 12,000 lost their jobs. Some got fired because they were (or had once been) members of the American Communist Party—which was perfectly legal. Others were merely suspected of being "Communist sympathizers." Often that conclusion was based on "guilt by association"—the person had friends or acquaintances with ties to communism.

Some of the most infamous episodes in the country's Communist witch-hunt took place in Congress. In 1947, the House Un-American Activities Committee (HUAC) began holding hearings to probe possible Communist influence in the movie industry. Ten screenwriters and directors refused to say whether they had Communist ties. The Hollywood Ten, as they came to be called, were eventually cited for contempt of Congress. They received jail sentences. They were also blacklisted. That meant no one in the entertainment industry would hire them.

HUAC's investigation continued for years. And the entertainment industry's blacklist expanded dramatically. It came to include more than 300 directors, producers, writers, actors, musicians, and radio journalists. Many of the blacklisted people had, on principle, refused to answer questions about their own political beliefs. Many had refused to name friends or acquaintances who might be Communists.

As HUAC's hearings went on in the House of Representatives, anti-communist hysteria engulfed the Senate. It began with a February

1950 speech by an obscure senator from Wisconsin. During that speech, Senator Joseph McCarthy waved a piece of paper. He said it contained a list of more than 200 known Communists working in the U.S. State Department. McCarthy didn't produce the list. And he soon changed key details of his story. But he rocketed to national prominence anyway.

Over the next four years, McCarthy railed constantly against what he said was widespread Communist influence in the government. He accused many people of disloyalty to the United States. He used a range of dirty tactics: rumors, charges made without evidence, half-truths and outright lies, guilt by association.

Senator Joseph McCarthy used investigations and government hearings to destroy the lives and careers of people he suspected of being Communists. His nasty tactics, known as "McCarthyism," were eventually discredited and his career ended in disgrace.

In 1954, public opinion finally turned against McCarthy and his tactics. His career was effectively ended when the Senate voted to censure (reprimand) him.

Interventions

The United States championed the principle of self-determination. It insisted that all peoples had the right to choose the government under which they would live. During the Cold War, though, the United States didn't always live up to its ideals. In their zeal to stop the spread of communism, American policy makers sometimes thwarted democracy in other countries.

The Eisenhower administration used covert, or secret, action to topple two democratically elected leaders. In 1953, the Central Intelligence Agency (CIA)—along with the British MI6 intelligence service—sponsored a coup in Iran. It ousted the prime minister, Mohammad Mossadegh, and restored to power the Shah (king). "It was the potential . . . to leave Iran open to Soviet aggression" that motivated the removal of Mossadegh, noted a CIA report declassified in 2013.

A 1954 coup masterminded by the CIA overthrew the leader of a Central American country. The Eisenhower administration claimed Guatemalan president Jacobo Arbenz Guzmán was secretly a Communist. But his removal may have had more to do with business interests. Arbenz's land reform policies threatened the profits of a powerful American corporation, the United Fruit Company.

In Vietnam, the United States didn't overthrow an elected leader. But it did stop democratic elections from taking place. The elections, scheduled for 1956, were supposed to unify North and South Vietnam. They'd been agreed to in a peace treaty ending Vietnam's war of independence from France. But the Eisenhower administration recognized that the Communist leader Ho Chi Minh would almost certainly win the elections. The administration's decision to block the vote set the United States on a tragic course.

Unrest in the Eastern Bloc

In 1955, West Germany was admitted to NATO. In response, the Soviet Union organized its own military and political alliance. Known as the Warsaw Pact, it included Albania (which would later withdraw), Bulgaria, Czechoslovakia, East Germany, Hungary, Poland, Romania, and the USSR. The Warsaw Pact solidified Soviet control over the Communist *Eastern bloc* nations. But that control would soon be challenged.

In late October 1956, a popular uprising against Soviet domination swept across Hungary. Imre Nagy, who'd become Hungary's prime minister amid the unrest, declared that his country would withdraw from the Warsaw Pact. He asked the Soviet Union to remove its forces from Hungary. At first, Moscow agreed. But that decision was soon reversed. "If we depart from Hungary," declared Soviet premier Nikita Khrushchev at a high-level Kremlin meeting, "it will give a great boost to the Americans, English, and French—the imperialists. They will perceive it as weakness on our part and will go onto the offensive."

On November 4, Soviet forces invaded Hungary. They brutally put down the Hungarian Revolution, killing at least 2,500 people. Nagy was executed and replaced with a hard-line Communist. An estimated 200,000 Hungarians fled the country.

SPUTNIK AND THE SPACE RACE

On October 4, 1957, the Soviet Union launched the first man-made satellite. *Sputnik 1* orbited the earth for three months.

Among many Americans, the reaction approached panic. It appeared that the United States had fallen behind the USSR in science and technology. And rockets developed to send satellites into space could be adapted to deliver nuclear bombs to cities.

In 1958, Congress authorized the establishment of the National Aeronautics and Space Administration. NASA's mission was to coordinate U.S. spaceflight efforts.

President Kennedy set the terms of the so-called space race in May 1961. In a speech before a joint session of Congress, he announced that the United States would pursue the goal of sending a person safely to the moon by the end of the decade.

At first, the USSR seemed more likely to achieve that feat. In April 1961, Soviet cosmonaut Yuri Gagarin became the first person in space and the first person to orbit the earth. But the U.S. space program soon overtook that of the USSR.

In July 1969, Apollo 11 astronauts Neil Armstrong and Buzz Aldrin became the first humans on the moon. Over the next three years, the United States conducted five additional lunar landings. The Soviet Union never sent anyone to the moon.

Soviet premier Nikita S. Khrushchev (right) meets with Fidel Castro of Cuba at the United Nations in September 1960.

Khrushchev had unwittingly encouraged the uprising in Hungary, as well as unrest in Poland. Following the death of Joseph Stalin in 1953, he'd emerged from a two-year power struggle as the USSR's top leader. In February 1956, Khrushchev had given a speech in which he severely criticized Stalin. Some people living in the Eastern bloc countries thought that meant the USSR was prepared to give them greater freedoms. They were wrong.

In his February speech, Khrushchev had also rejected Stalin's belief that war with the United States was inevitable. He said that Communist and capitalist countries could coexist peacefully.

Yet Khrushchev had a knack for instigating crises. By 1958, large numbers of Germans were leaving East Berlin for the greater freedom and prosperity of West Berlin. Khrushchev regarded that as an embarrassment to communism. He ordered all U.S., British, and French forces out of West Berlin. President Eisenhower stood firm, however.

In 1961, Khrushchev tried to intimidate a new U.S. president into withdrawing from West Berlin. He gave American forces six months to leave the city. But President John F. Kennedy sent 150,000 reserve troops to Europe for a possible fight. Khrushchev backed down. Finally, in August 1961, the East German government erected the Berlin Wall. It ended the crisis by keeping Germans from moving between East and West Berlin. The wall became a powerful symbol of Communist repression.

TEXT-DEPENDENT QUESTIONS

1. What was NSC-68?
2. What was the Warsaw Pact? How many of its members can you name?
3. What was *Sputnik*? Why did it alarm Americans?

RESEARCH PROJECT

In the name of thwarting communism, the United States helped overthrow elected leaders in Iran (1953) and Guatemala (1954). Choose one of these countries and research what happened there in the aftermath of the coup. Who replaced the ousted leader? How were ordinary citizens affected? Do you think the country might be different today if not for the U.S. intervention? In what ways?

Chapter 4:

TO THE BRINK

During the 1960 presidential campaign, John F. Kennedy was highly critical of the Eisenhower administration. He blasted the administration for the "missile gap." Echoing a widespread belief, Kennedy said the Soviet Union had built a lead in the development of intercontinental ballistic missiles, or ICBMs.

First deployed in 1959, ICBMs could deliver nuclear warheads to targets thousands of miles away. Unlike bomber aircraft, they couldn't be shot down.

As the U.S. and Soviet Union built up their nuclear arsenals, the danger of a nuclear war increased. (Left) An American Titan II intercontinental ballistic missile (ICBM) is launched from an underground silo. The Titan II carried a warhead that could destroy a city. (Right) Soviet soldiers stand near a truck equipped to launch a smaller nuclear missile, for use on the battlefield against enemy troops.

WORDS TO UNDERSTAND IN THIS CHAPTER

brinkmanship—the practice of pushing a dangerous situation to the limit of safety, in order to obtain concessions from an adversary.

détente (pronounced day-tahnt)—the relaxation of tensions between nations.

West—in Cold War contexts, the United States and its allies.

Many Americans feared that Soviet leaders might be tempted to use their ICBM advantage to launch a nuclear strike against the United States. But in fact, the USSR didn't have an ICBM advantage. To the extent there was a missile gap, it favored the United States. Eisenhower knew this from the top-secret U-2 spy plane program.

A New Strategy

Upon taking office, Kennedy also learned that the missile gap didn't exist. But he and his advisers still had broad objections to Eisenhower's defense policies. They rejected the doctrine of massive retaliation. They thought nuclear *brinkmanship* was reckless. The United States, Kennedy believed, could never use nuclear weapons except in response to a nuclear attack.

The Kennedy administration pressed for increased military spending, much of it for a buildup of conventional forces. That would be necessary to pursue the administration's "flexible response" strategy. The goal was to give policy makers appropriate options for dealing with the wide range of possible Communist threats. A limited threat, Kennedy believed, should draw a robust but limited response. Above all, the United States should avoid escalating any crisis into a nuclear showdown.

Ironically, Kennedy would find himself confronting exactly that situation. The trouble centered on Cuba.

The Bay of Pigs

In 1959, a revolution overthrew Cuba's dictator, and Fidel Castro took power. Castro cultivated a close relationship with the Soviet Union, which drew the ire of American officials. In 1960, President Eisenhower approved a secret CIA plan to oust Castro. The CIA trained some 1,400 Cuban exiles for an invasion.

Preparations for the invasion were in the final stages when John F. Kennedy became president. Kennedy approved the mission.

On April 17, 1961, the Cuban exiles landed in Cuba at a place called the Bay of Pigs. But almost nothing went according to plan. Within two days, Castro's forces had routed the invaders.

The Bay of Pigs fiasco caused international embarrassment for the new American president. But Kennedy didn't give up on trying to get rid of Castro, who soon announced that he was a Communist. The president authorized Operation Mongoose. The covert program organized guerrilla raids in Cuba. The CIA also tried to assassinate Castro.

Castro appealed to the Soviet Union for help. Nikita Khrushchev sent a large quantity of weapons and 40,000 Soviet combat troops to Cuba. He also made a very dangerous decision: to station Soviet nuclear missiles on the island.

The Cuban Missile Crisis

On October 16, 1962, Kennedy was informed that a U-2 reconnaissance flight had photographed a Soviet missile base under construction in the jungle near San Cristóbal, Cuba. Other U-2 flights would discover more bases as well as ballistic missiles. Those missiles were clearly offensive weapons. They could deliver nuclear warheads to East Coast cities with virtually no warning, as Cuba is just 90 miles from the southern tip of

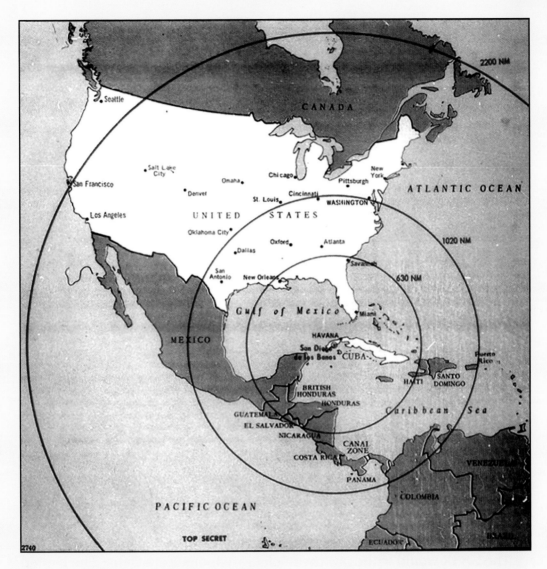

This map prepared by the CIA in 1962 shows how missiles fired from Cuba could strike nearly any city in the continental United States.

Florida. Kennedy considered that risk unacceptable.

The Joint Chiefs of Staff, made up of senior military leaders, pressed the president to approve a massive bombing campaign and invasion of Cuba. Worried about possible Soviet retaliation, Kennedy balked. Instead, he ordered a naval blockade (officially called a quarantine). The aim was to prevent Soviet ships from delivering parts needed to make the missiles operational.

On October 22, the president first informed the country of the developing crisis in a televised address. He also sent a letter to Khrushchev saying the United States couldn't accept nuclear weapons in Cuba. The Soviet premier responded angrily. "You, Mr. President, have flung a challenge at us," Khrushchev wrote in a letter to Kennedy. "Who asked you to do this? By what right did you do this?" Khrushchev refused to remove the missiles.

Days passed, and the standoff continued. The Strategic Air Command (SAC)—the arm of the U.S. Air Force responsible for strategic nuclear weapons—was placed on high alert.

An almost unbearable tension settled over the country. Many Americans went to bed each night wondering if they'd be alive the next morning.

Events nearly spiraled out of control on October 27. That day, a Soviet surface-to-air missile shot down a U-2 spy plane over Cuba. The pilot was killed. President Kennedy refused to order immediate military action, as the Joint Chiefs advocated. But to officials like Secretary of Defense Robert McNamara, an invasion of Cuba now seemed almost inevitable.

A peaceful way out of the crisis emerged on the night of the 27th, however. At a secret meeting, Attorney General Robert Kennedy and Soviet ambassador Anatoly Dobrynin worked out the outlines of an agreement. The USSR would withdraw the nuclear weapons from Cuba. The United States would promise not to invade the island, and American intermediate-range ballistic missiles in Turkey would later be removed.

The foundation of mutually assured destruction was the so-called strategic nuclear triad: land-based missiles, submarine-launched missiles, and bomber planes. The three separate delivery systems made it virtually impossible that any attack could destroy enough warheads to prevent devastating retaliation.

A VERY CLOSE CALL

During the Cuban missile crisis, the United States and the Soviet Union came close to a thermonuclear war. No one knew just how close until 1989. That year, Soviet sources revealed something American officials had been unaware of in 1962: that Soviet forces in Cuba had tactical (battlefield) nuclear weapons, along with at least a half-dozen operational medium-range ballistic missiles (MRBMs). What's more, Soviet field commanders had the authority to use the tactical nuclear weapons without prior approval from the Kremlin.

Today, many experts think that if President Kennedy had ordered an invasion of Cuba, as the Joint Chiefs urged, Soviet forces would have used their tactical nuclear weapons. And many also believe the MRBMs would have been launched as well. Those missiles could have incinerated cities as far north as Washington, D.C.

In the White House, the resolution of the crisis was greeted with jubilation and an intense sense of relief. Millions of ordinary Americans shared those feelings. Some of the nation's top military leaders did not. The head of the U.S. Navy told President Kennedy he'd been duped by the Kremlin. General Curtis LeMay, chief of staff of the U.S. Air Force, sneered that Kennedy had accepted "the greatest defeat in our history."

MAD and the Quest for Deterrence

At the time of the Cuban missile crisis, top American military leaders believed a nuclear war was winnable. LeMay, for example, claimed that "the Soviet Union could have been obliterated without more than normal expectable SAC losses on our side." The two superpowers had comparable numbers of nuclear warheads. But while the United States could hit the USSR with about 3,500 atomic and hydrogen bombs, the Soviet Union could deliver only about 300 to 350 of its bombs. If the United States launched a massive first strike—as LeMay openly discussed—most of the USSR's nuclear weapons might be destroyed before they could be used.

Both sides dramatically expanded their nuclear arsenals, and their delivery systems, in the years after the Cuban missile crisis. Even the most hawkish generals now recognized that a nuclear war with the USSR couldn't be won.

The superpowers sought to deter each other through mutually assured destruction, or MAD. Each side had enough nuclear weapons to wipe out its adversary many times over. Regardless of which side launched its weapons first, both countries would in the end be annihilated. Thus, according to the logic of MAD, no sane leader would ever contemplate a nuclear attack.

Even as the doctrine of MAD became firmly established, political leaders sought to lessen the risks of nuclear weapons. The Limited Test Ban Treaty—signed in 1963 by the United States, the USSR, and the United Kingdom—was a modest step. According to the treaty, all future nuclear tests had to be conducted underground.

The Nuclear Non-Proliferation Treaty (NPT) was a milestone. Hammered out in the UN, the NPT went into effect in 1970. It was signed by 190 nations. Five of them—the United States, the USSR, the UK, France, and China—already had nuclear weapons. They promised to work toward nuclear disarmament. The other 185 nations committed to never developing nuclear weapons.

The Vietnam War

American efforts to contain the spread of communism in Southeast Asia drew the country step by step into a costly and controversial war. President Eisenhower had said that if Vietnam became Communist, its neighbors would fall like dominoes. The Eisenhower administration sent aid and U.S. military advisers to prop up the anticommunist government of South Vietnam.

The Kennedy administration increased the number of advisers, from about 900 in 1960 to 16,000 by 1963. The advisers were supposed to train

American infantry soldiers descend a hill into the jungle of Vietnam, November 1967. Like other conflicts during the Cold War, American forces became involved in an effort to halt the spread of Communism.

the South Vietnamese army to fight the Vietcong—Communist guerrillas supported by North Vietnam. But some of the Americans inevitably went into battle alongside their South Vietnamese allies.

By 1965, during the administration of President Lyndon B. Johnson, the United States had taken on a full and open combat role in Vietnam. That year, more than 180,000 American servicemen were fighting in the Vietnam War. They battled the Vietcong and North Vietnamese regular

THE PRAGUE SPRING

During the first half of 1968, Czechoslovakia experimented with a less repressive form of communism. This period, known as the Prague Spring, was brought about largely by Czechoslovakia's Communist Party chairman, Alexander Dubček. Dubček said he wanted to create "socialism with a human face." That meant doing away with press censorship. It meant allowing civil liberties unknown in the Eastern bloc, including freedom of expression and freedom of movement. It meant tolerating non-Communist organizations and planning for a multiparty political system.

Soviet leaders, worried that the Czechoslovakian reforms might spread to other Eastern bloc countries, decided to put an end to the Prague Spring. On August 20–21, 1968, about a quarter million Warsaw Pact troops invaded Czechoslovakia. Dubček and other reformers were arrested and hard-line Communists placed in power. In justifying the invasion, Soviet leader Leonid Brezhnev said, "When external and internal forces hostile to socialism try to turn the development of a given socialist country in the direction of the restoration of the capitalist system . . . this is no longer merely a problem for that country's people, but a common problem, the concern of all socialist countries." The supposed right of the Soviet Union to uphold socialism in another country through force became known as the Brezhnev Doctrine.

soldiers. American troop strength peaked in 1968 at more than half a million.

By that time, the American people were bitterly divided over the war. Elected president in 1968, Richard Nixon hoped to bring the Vietnam War to a quick conclusion. But that proved difficult. U.S. combat forces weren't withdrawn from Vietnam until 1973, after more than 58,000 American deaths. South Vietnam fell to the Communists in 1975.

Cold War Thaw

Nixon sought better relations with the USSR. He pursued a policy called détente, meaning a lessening of tensions between nations.

In February 1972, Nixon became the first U.S. president to travel to the People's Republic of China. He hoped to get the Kremlin's attention by cultivating closer ties with China. Relations between the world's two largest Communist nations had been strained since the late 1950s. Soviet leaders, Nixon reasoned, would be more open to détente if they were worried about China aligning with the United States.

Nixon went to Moscow in May 1972. There, he and Soviet premier Leonid Brezhnev signed agreements that had emerged from the first Strategic

U.S. President Richard Nixon and Soviet Premier Leonid Brezhnev meet at the White House, 1973. During the 1970s, the American and Soviet governments pursued a policy known as détente, which enabled the two superpowers to sign several agreements to reduce their arsenals of nuclear weapons.

Arms Limitation Talks (SALT I), begun in 1969. One of the agreements capped, at 1972 levels, the number of ballistic missiles each country was allowed to have. The agreement would remain in effect for five years. Meanwhile, a second round of negotiations, SALT II, would seek reductions in nuclear weapons.

Détente continued under Nixon's successor, President Gerald Ford. In 1975, the United States and the USSR—along with Canada and every country in Europe except Albania—signed the Helsinki Accords. The agreement formally recognized Europe's post–World War II borders. That was controversial in the *West* because it accepted the Soviet Union's 1940 seizure of the Baltic States (Estonia, Latvia, and Lithuania). But the Helsinki Accords also required governments to respect the human rights of their citizens. Further, the accords promoted cultural and scientific exchanges between the West and the Eastern bloc. Those measures would eventually play a role in opening up the closed societies of Eastern Europe.

Hot Spots

In spite of some progress, détente didn't mean the Cold War was about to end. Developing countries continued to be battlegrounds in the superpowers' struggle. Angola, in southwestern Africa, was an especially brutal example. The USSR and the United States armed rival sides in a complicated civil war that followed Angola's independence from Portugal in 1975. Cuban troops fought on the side of Angola's Communist faction.

A 1977–78 conflict between Ethiopia and Somalia also drew the attention of the superpowers. The United States supported Somalia, while the USSR supported Ethiopia. Once again, Cuban troops took a direct combat role.

If one event killed détente, though, it was the USSR's Christmas Day 1979 invasion of its southern neighbor Afghanistan. In the wake of the invasion, President Jimmy Carter asked Congress not to ratify the SALT II Treaty. Carter and Leonid Brezhnev had signed the treaty six months earlier.

The Kremlin had decided to invade Afghanistan in order to prop up a Communist regime there. Instead, the invasion hastened the collapse of the Soviet Union itself.

 ## TEXT-DEPENDENT QUESTIONS

1. Where is the Bay of Pigs? What happened there?
2. What does "MAD" stand for?
3. What was the "Prague Spring"?

 ## RESEARCH PROJECT

Read about either John F. Kennedy, Nikita Khrushchev, or Fidel Castro. Then write a short biography.

Chapter 5:

THE FINAL YEARS

Citizens of the Soviet Union had a joke about their government's management of the economy. "They pretend to pay us," the punch line went, "and we pretend to work."

The joke contained more than a grain of truth. Wages for most workers were, in fact, very low. But since the government would pay them regardless of their performance, people had little incentive to work hard.

Residents of East and West Berlin cross though the Berlin Wall at Potsdamer Platz, November 1989. The fall of the Wall showed that Communism was collapsing. East and West Germany reunited as a single nation in 1990, and the Soviet Union itself ceased to exist in December 1991, breaking into 15 separate states.

WORDS TO UNDERSTAND IN THIS CHAPTER

glasnost—a Soviet reform policy allowing more open discussion of political and social issues and a freer press.

perestroika—a Soviet reform policy whose goal was to restructure the USSR's government and economy.

Low worker productivity was just one of the weaknesses in the USSR's economy. Central planning led to the inefficient use of resources. Innovation was stifled. Soviet industry was slow to adopt new technologies.

By the early 1970s, the Soviet economy had stagnated. With each passing year, it lost ground to the more dynamic capitalist economies of the United States and other Western nations. Overall, the Soviet people had a low standard of living.

Accompanying the economic stagnation, scholars of the USSR have noted, was a broader stagnation of Soviet society. Citizens were weary and demoralized. They were fed up with the Communist Party's corruption. They hated the way the government repressed them. They didn't believe what their leaders said. Increasingly, they questioned the legitimacy of Communist rule itself.

In 1983, a diplomat returning to the USSR after a decade overseas summed up the profound disaffection of the Soviet people. "Enough! We cannot live like this any longer. Everything must be done in a new way. . . . There has come an understanding that it is simply impossible to live as we lived before—intolerably, humiliatingly."

Reformer

Mikhail S. Gorbachev believed he could save Soviet communism. But major changes would be needed. Shortly after he became the USSR's top leader in March 1985, Gorbachev started a program of reforms. It was called *perestroika*, meaning "restructuring."

The restructuring Gorbachev had in mind was both economic and political. To make the Soviet economy more competitive, Gorbachev allowed some failing state enterprises to go bankrupt. He permitted some farmers to lease land for their own use. He introduced a limited degree of private business ownership.

Politically, *perestroika* involved the gradual introduction of limited democracy. Under a policy known as *glasnost* ("openness"), Soviet citizens were allowed greater freedom of expression. And the news media, which previously had been under the complete control of the state, became more independent.

Reagan Doctrine

Gorbachev's efforts to reform the Soviet system were complicated by the Cold War. In 1981, Ronald Reagan had become president of the United States. Reagan referred to the USSR as an "evil empire" and called communism a "sad, bizarre chapter in human history whose last pages are even now being written."

Reagan departed from the strategy of containment, which had guided U.S. presidents since the onset of the Cold War. Containment was defensive—it sought to stop the spread of communism. Reagan introduced an offensive element. He called for communism to be rolled back in places where Communists had recently come to power. Under the Reagan Doctrine, as this idea was called, the United States armed rebels fighting Soviet-supported regimes in Afghanistan, Angola, and Nicaragua.

Afghanistan presented by far the most serious challenge to the USSR. The 1979 Soviet invasion had turned into a quagmire. Despite having more than 100,000 troops in Afghanistan, the Soviet Union was unable to quell rebel fighters. As Soviet casualties mounted, the war became

U.S. president Ronald Reagan (left) meets Soviet general secretary Mikhail Gorbachev in Switzerland, November 1985. During the 1980s, Gorbachev implemented new policies that allowed greater freedom in Soviet society. These would lead to the end of the Cold War and to the breakup of the Soviet Union in 1991.

more and more unpopular inside the USSR. But Soviet forces wouldn't be withdrawn until 1989.

In spite of the Reagan Doctrine, Gorbachev sought better relations with the United States. He advocated nuclear disarmament, a goal President Reagan shared. Not surprisingly, an agreement to get rid of all nuclear weapons proved elusive. But in 1987, the United States and the USSR concluded a treaty that eliminated intermediate-range nuclear missiles. And in 1991, the superpowers signed the Strategic Arms Reduction Treaty (START). It significantly cut each country's nuclear arsenal.

Breakup of the Eastern Bloc

In 1988, Mikhail Gorbachev assured the Soviet people that his reform policies were around to stay. "Through democratization, economic reform and changes in the political system," Gorbachev said in a nationally televised speech, "*perestroika* will be irreversible."

People in Eastern Europe wondered what the changes in the Soviet Union meant for them. Could they demand reforms in their own countries? Or would the USSR crush any serious opposition movements? That's what had always happened before. Most recently, in 1981–82, Poland's government had squelched the Solidarity trade-union movement on orders from the Kremlin.

But in 1988, Poland was rocked by a series of labor strikes. Workers demanded that the government legalize Solidarity.

In March 1989, the first competitive elections in the history of the USSR were held. Voters elected representatives to a new national legislature, the Congress of People's Deputies. Many Communist Party candidates were defeated.

The following month, Poland's government legalized Solidarity. In parliamentary elections held in June, Solidarity candidates won an overwhelming victory.

In July, at the Warsaw Pact's annual summit, Gorbachev made clear that the Brezhnev Doctrine was dead. The Soviet Union wasn't going to intervene in the affairs of Eastern European nations.

A wave of East Germans began trying to get to West Germany. It started after Hungary opened its border with Austria and permitted East German tourists to cross. Soon thousands of East Germans sought asylum at the West German embassy in Prague, Czechoslovakia. East Germany sealed its borders with other Warsaw Pact countries. Protests broke out across East Germany. Hoping to save Communist rule, party officials replaced longtime leader Erich Honecker in October. But the protests only intensified.

The East German government decided to allow citizens to travel to the West with official permission. But on November 9, when the new rules were to go into effect, hundreds of thousands of East Berliners surged through checkpoints into West Berlin. The Berlin Wall had fallen.

In rapid succession, the Communist governments of Eastern Europe fell. By late November 1989, a peaceful revolution had toppled Czechoslovakia's regime. The Communists were ousted from East Germany in December. That same month, Bulgaria's Communist Party gave up its monopoly on power, and Romania's dictator was violently overthrown. Hungarians elected a non-Communist government in April 1990. Six months later, East and West Germany were reunited.

Collapse of the USSR

In the Soviet Union, perestroika and glasnost had some unforeseen effects. One was to unleash long-suppressed ethnic tensions.

Russians had always dominated the USSR. Outside of the Russian Soviet Federative Republic, though, ethnic Russians constituted a minority of the population. Other groups harbored deep resentments. Some had been brutally treated by the Soviet government, particularly under Joseph Stalin.

East and West Germans converge at the newly created opening in the Berlin Wall after a crane removed a section of the structure beside the Brandenburg Gate, December 1989.

With Gorbachev's reforms, people in the various Soviet socialist republics began openly decrying Russia's dominance. They demanded greater cultural and political rights. The Baltic States led the way. By 1990, Estonia, Latvia, and Lithuania had all announced their independence from the USSR. The Soviet Union, however, didn't recognize any separation.

Gorbachev's solution to the growing problem of ethnic nationalism was to promote a new Union Treaty. Under the agreement, the central government would remain in charge of the military and of foreign policy. But the republics would become largely independent.

The signing ceremony for the Union Treaty was scheduled for August 20, 1991. On the 19th, however, hard-line members of the Soviet Communist Party placed Gorbachev under house arrest. Calling themselves the Committee on the State of Emergency, they said they were now in charge of the USSR.

But massive crowds took to the streets of Moscow to protest the coup. Army units ordered to break up the protests refused to do so. By August 22, the coup had collapsed. Gorbachev returned, but he was effectively powerless.

On December 25, 1991, the Soviet Union officially dissolved, with Russia and 15 other independent countries emerging in its place. The adversary with which the United States and its allies had contended since the late 1940s was no more. The West had won the Cold War.

 ## TEXT-DEPENDENT QUESTIONS

1. How did the Reagan Doctrine change the policy of containment?
2. In what year did the Eastern bloc break up?
3. Why did the August 1991 coup attempt against Gorbachev fail?

 ## RESEARCH PROJECT

Choose something about the Cold War that interests you. It could be a person, a country, an incident, a weapons system, the space race, even a movie or a story about the period. Find out more. Then make a list of what you were surprised to learn about the topic.

CHRONOLOGY

1946   The "Long Telegram" helps define the American strategy of containment.

1947   President Truman outlines the Truman Doctrine; Congress approves aid to Greece and Turkey. The American, British, and French occupation zones in Germany are combined. HUAC begins hearings on possible Communist influence in the entertainment industry.

1948   The USSR sponsors a coup in Czechoslovakia. The Marshall Plan, aimed at rebuilding Europe, begins. The Soviet Union blockades West Berlin; in response, the United States organizes an airlift.

1949   NATO is founded (April 4). The USSR ends the blockade of West Berlin. West Germany is founded (May 23). The Soviet Union successfully tests an atomic bomb in August. The People's Republic of China is founded (Oct. 1). East Germany is founded (Oct. 7).

1950   The Korean War begins in June.

1952   The United States tests the first hydrogen bomb (Nov. 1).

1953   In June, an armistice ends the fighting in the Korean War. The USSR tests a hydrogen bomb in August. The CIA sponsors a successful coup in Iran.

1954   A CIA-sponsored coup ousts Guatemala's president, Jacobo Arbenz.

1955   The Warsaw Pact is founded.

1956   Soviet forces put down the Hungarian Revolution in November.

1957   The Soviet Union launches the world's first artificial satellite, Sputnik 1.

1959	The United States and the Soviet Union deploy ICBMs.
1961	The Bay of Pigs invasion fails. The Berlin Wall is erected.
1962	In October, the Cuban missile crisis brings the United States and the Soviet Union to the brink of war.
1963	The Limited Test Ban Treaty is signed.
1965	U.S. involvement in the Vietnam War escalates dramatically.
1968	Warsaw Pact forces invade Czechoslovakia and put an end to the "Prague Spring."
1970	The Nuclear Non-Proliferation Treaty goes into effect.
1972	President Richard Nixon travels to China. The USSR and the United States agree to cap the number of ballistic missiles they have under SALT I.
1975	South Vietnam falls, two years after the withdrawal of American combat troops.
1979	The Soviet Union invades Afghanistan in December.
1985	Mikhail Gorbachev becomes the USSR's top leader, launches reform program.
1989	The first competitive elections in the history of the USSR are held (March). In Polish elections held in June, Communist candidates are trounced by Solidarity. The Berlin Wall falls (Nov. 9). A peaceful revolution topples Czechoslovakia's government in November. In December, Communist regimes are replaced in East Germany and Romania. Bulgaria's Communist Party announces an end to its monopoly on power.
1990	Hungarians elect a noncommunist government. The Baltic States agitate for independence. Germany reunites.
1991	In August, Gorbachev is placed under house arrest in an attempted coup. The coup fails after massive demonstrations. On December 25, the Soviet Union officially dissolves.

CHAPTER NOTES

p.11: "an iron curtain . . ." Winston S. Churchill, "Iron Curtain Speech," March 5, 1946. *Modern History Sourcebook*. http://www.fordham. edu/halsall/mod/churchill-iron.asp

p. 11: "the right of all people . . ." The Yalta Conference. The Avalon Project: Documents in Law, History and Diplomacy. http://avalon.law. yale.edu/wwii/yalta.asp

p. 11: "He is straightforward . . ." Robert Gellately, *Stalin's Curse: Battling for Communism in War and Cold War* (Oxford, UK: Oxford University Press, 2013), p. 165.

p. 14: "in the last analysis . . ." Melvyn P. Leffler and Odd Arne Vestad (editors), *The Cambridge History of the Cold War,* Volume 1: Origins (Cambridge, UK: Cambridge University Press, 2010), p. 70.

p. 16: "undoubtedly [the] greatest . . ." Telegram, George Kennan to George Marshall ["Long Telegram"], February 22, 1946. https:// www.trumanlibrary.org/whistlestop/study_collections/coldwar/ documents/pdf/6-6.pdf

p. 19: "aggressive movements," Truman Doctrine: President Harry S. Truman's Address Before a Joint Session of Congress, March 12, 1947. The Avalon Project: Documents in Law, History and Diplomacy. http://avalon.law.yale.edu/20th_century/trudoc.asp

p. 19: "terror and oppression . . ." Ibid.

p. 19: "I believe that it must . . ." Ibid.

p. 20: "World communism is like . . ." Telegram, George Kennan to George Marshall. https://www.trumanlibrary.org/whistlestop/ study_collections/coldwar/documents/pdf/6-6.pdf

p. 26: "to impose its absolute . . ." "A Report to the National Security Council—NSC 68," April 12, 1950 [p. 4]. https://www.trumanlibrary.org/whistlestop/study_collections/coldwar/documents/ pdf/10-1.pdf

p. 29: "The ability to get . . ." Howard Jones, *Crucible of Power: A History of American Foreign Relations from 1945* (Lanham, MD: Rowman & Littlefield, 2009) , p. 63.

p. 32: "It was the potential . . ." J. Dana Stuster, "Mapped: The 7 Governments the U.S. Has Overthrown," *Foreign Policy* (Aug. 19, 2013). http://www.foreignpolicy.com/articles/2013/08/19/ map_7_confirmed_cia_backed_coups

p. 33:　"If we depart . . ." DOCUMENT NO. 6 Working Notes and Attached Extract from the Minutes of the CPSU CC Presidium Meeting, October 31, 1956. The National Security Archive, George Washington University. http://www2.gwu.edu/~nsarchiv/NSAEBB/NSAEBB76/doc6.pdf

p. 40:　"You, Mr. President, have flung . . ." Letter from Chairman Khrushchev to President Kennedy [October 24, 1962]. *Foreign Relations of the United States, 1961–1963*. Volume VI, Kennedy-Khrushchev Exchanges, Document 63. U.S. Department of State, Office of the Historian. https://history.state.gov/historicaldocuments/frus1961-63v06/d63

p. 41:　"the greatest defeat . . ." Robert Dallek, "JFK vs. the Military," *The Atlantic* (Sept. 10, 2013). http://www.theatlantic.com/magazine/archive/2013/08/jfk-vs-the-military/309496/?single_page=true

p. 41:　"the Soviet Union could . . ." Richard Rhodes, *Dark Sun: The Making of the Hydrogen Bomb* (New York: Simon & Schuster, 1995), p. 574.

p. 44:　"When external and internal . . ." Matthew J. Oimet, *The Rise and Fall of the Brezhnev Doctrine in Soviet Foreign Policy* (Chapel Hill: University of North Carolina Press, 2003) , p. 67.

p. 48:　"They pretend to pay . . ." Naomi Marcus, "What's in it for Me, Comrade?" *Mother Jones* (Oct. 1988): 30.

p. 49:　"Enough! We cannot live . . ." Leon Aron, "Everything You Think You Know About the Collapse of the Soviet Union Is Wrong," *Foreign Policy* (June 20, 2011). http://www.foreignpolicy.com/articles/2011/06/20/everything_you_think_you_know_about_the_collapse_of_the_soviet_union_is_wrong

p. 50:　"evil empire," Ronald Reagan, "Evil Empire" Speech (March 8, 1983). http://millercenter.org/president/speeches/speech-3409

p. 50:　"sad, bizarre chapter . . ." Ibid.

p. 52:　"Through democratization . . ." Thom Shanker, "Soviet Party Endorses Blueprint for Change," *Chicago Tribune*, July 8, 1988. http://articles.chicagotribune.com/1988-07-02/news/8801120226_1_soviet-leader-communist-party-reform

FURTHER READING

Beyer, Mark. *Nuclear Weapons and the Cold War*. New York: Rosen Publishing, 2004.

Fitzgerald, Stephanie. *McCarthyism: The Red Scare*. Mankato, MN: Compass Point Books, 2006.

Gaddis, John Lewis. *The Cold War: A New History*. New York: Penguin, 2006.

Mastny, Vojtech, and Zhu Liqun, eds. *The Legacy of the Cold War: Perspectives on Security, Cooperation, and Conflict*. Lanham, MD: Rowman & Littlefield, 2013.

Schier, Helga. *The Cuban Missile Crisis*. Edina, MN: ABDO, 2008.

Zubok, Vladislav M. *A Failed Empire: The Soviet Union in the Cold War from Stalin to Gorbachev*. Chapel Hill: University of North Carolina Press, 2009.

INTERNET RESOURCES

http://www.coldwar.org/

> The website of the Cold War Museum includes short entries on a variety of subjects, organized by decade.

http://www.trumanlibrary.org/whistlestop/study_ collections/coldwar/index.php

> "Ideological Foundations of the Cold War," an online resource from the Harry S. Truman Library and Museum, offers a timeline, photographs, documents, oral histories, and more.

http://www.loc.gov/exhibits/archives/sovi.html

> What did Soviet leaders think about the United States and the Cold War? "Revelations from the Russian Archives," an online exhibit maintained by the Library of Congress, includes Soviet-era documents that shed light on that question.

http://microsites.jfklibrary.org/cmc/

> A detailed examination of the Cuban missile crisis, from the John F. Kennedy Presidential Library and Museum.

INDEX

Numbers in **bold italics** refer to captions.

SERIES GLOSSARY

blockade—an effort to cut off supplies, war material, or communications by a particular area, by force or the threat of force.

guerrilla warfare—a type of warfare in which a small group of combatants, such as armed civilians, use hit-and-run tactics to fight a larger and less mobile traditional army. The purpose is to weaken an enemy's strength through small skirmishes, rather than fighting pitched battles where the guerrillas would be at a disadvantage.

intelligence—the analysis of information collected from various sources in order to provide guidance and direction to military commanders.

logistics—the planning and execution of movements by military forces, and the supply of those forces.

salient—a pocket or bulge in a fortified line or battle line that projects into enemy territory.

siege—a military blockade of a city or fortress, with the intent of conquering it at a later stage.

tactics—the science and art of organizing a military force, and the techniques for using military units and their weapons to defeat an enemy in battle.